CHRISTIANS IN AN UNCHRISTIAN SOCIETY

ERNEST FREMONT TITTLE

Author of
Jesus after Nineteen Centuries
A World that Cannot Be Shaken
A Way of Life

Fourth Printing

Price 50 cents

HAZEN BOOKS ON RELIGION
The Edward W. Hazen Foundation, Inc.
Distributed by
ASSOCIATION PRESS
347 Madison Avenue
NEW YORK

A Note about The Hazen Books on Religion

THE purpose of this series is to present simply, compactly and inexpensively a number of the best available interpretations of the Christian philosophy as a guide to Christian living today.

The series is sponsored by the Edward W. Hazen Foundation. The responsibility for selecting the titles and authors and for planning the manufacture and distribution of the volumes rests with the following committee: John C. Bennett (chairman), Wilbur Davies, Georgia Harkness, S. M. Keeny, Benson Y. Landis, Mrs. W. W. Rockwell, William L. Savage, George Stewart, Henry P. Van Dusen, and a representative of the Edward W. Hazen Foundation. The responsibility for the subject matter of the volumes rests with the authors alone.

The following twelve volumes comprise the series:

Christianity—and Our World. By John C. Bennett. (Nine printings)
Jesus. By Mary Ely Lyman. (Seven printings)
God. By Walter Horton. (Five printings)
Religious Living. By Georgia Harkness. (Eight printings)
Toward a World Christian Fellowship. By Kenneth Scott Latourette. (Three printings)
Prayer and Worship. By Douglas Steere. (Five printings)
The Church. By George Stewart. (Three printings)
Christians in an Unchristian Society. By Ernest Fremont Tittle. (Three printings)
What Is Man? By Robert L. Calhoun. (Three printings)
Christian Faith and Democracy. By Gregory Vlastos. (Four printings)
The Bible. By Walter Russell Bowie. (Three printings)
Reality and Religion. By Henry P. Van Dusen. (Two printings)

The publication of these books is a co-operative, non-profit enterprise for everybody concerned.

Printed in the United States of America
Fourth Printing, May, 1945

ALLIED PRINTING TRADES UNION LABEL COUNCIL NEW YORK 145

To My Son's Children

Sara Lynn Tittle

David Ernest Fremont Tittle

Who, I Hope, Will Help to Create a

Better Society

CONTENTS

FOREWORD

The world is out of joint. What, if anything, can be done about it? This book is based upon the conviction that *much* can be done about it, provided that men are willing to avail themselves of the power and wisdom of God. Chapter I presents the ground for this conviction. Chapter II is addressed to the question, "What kind of world are we now called of God to seek after?" Chapter III maintains that only Christianity, in view of its faith and aims and methods, can hope to produce social changes that are desirable and enduring. Chapter IV undertakes to describe and appraise various attitudes that, historically, Christians have taken toward their world. This last chapter might logically have been the first. It may properly be read first by students who recognize the value of a historical approach to any issue that is really a matter of life and death.

CHAPTER I

GOD IN HISTORY

Is there any real hope of a better world? May we venture to look forward to a time when the institutions of society will at least offer no resistance to the human spirit in its attempt to rise above sensuality, greed, and cruelty; when the practices by which man secures his daily bread will not interfere with any desire he may have to love his neighbor as himself; and when his membership in a nation, to which he is bound by strong ties of tradition and affection, will not prevent him from cherishing a lively concern for the welfare of other nations?

The present outlook, it must be confessed, is not very encouraging. European observers remark upon the optimism that is still to be found in the United States, where, as one of them has said, "Christians still believe in the efficacy of constructive effort."[1] A European, this same observer declares, "cannot help be somewhat suspicious" of any belief "in the value, the power, and the efficacy of human or Christian efforts" to improve the world. It is, apparently, a fact that in continental Europe almost everywhere Christians have become passive in the presence of threatening disaster. They will not consent to deny their faith. Rather than do that, they will suffer the loss of all things. But they do not suppose that there is much, if anything, that they can do about the external order of the world. They cherish the hope, nursed by early Christians, of a divine interference from without our bourne of time and place; yet as events move on toward apparent catastrophe and nothing happens to divert their course, they feel ever more constrained to suppose that a world that has sinned can now expect nothing save the just but awful retribution of God. Nor do they suppose that the social conditions of human life on earth will ever be very

[1] See Adolph Keller's article in *Christendom,* Spring, 1938, p. 221.

much better than they now are. As they see it, any hopeful view of the future of this world is, to say the least of it, pathetically superficial. Indeed, they are not a little inclined to brush it aside as being quite unworthy of any serious consideration.

What is the explanation of so great a divergence from a common faith as that which now appears between Christians who believe in "the efficacy of constructive effort" and Christians who believe that human effort to improve the world is futile and foolish? It is tempting, because easy, to suppose that it is largely a matter of geography: American Christians live in a land that is three thousand miles away from that boiling cauldron of hates and fears which is the European inheritance; and the land they live in is overflowing with oil and iron and other natural resources. But this explanation, although there is, no doubt, some truth in it, is certainly no adequate account of the situation. There are Christians in America who are by no means convinced of the possibility of any radical kind of social improvement. There are Christians in Europe who, notwithstanding the desperate character of their situation, still believe in "the efficacy of constructive effort." Is it, after all, quite fair to assume that human faith is largely, if not wholly, conditioned by circumstances? Is it true that the pessimism that is characteristic of European Christianity, as also the optimism that colors American Christianity, is but the natural, if not the inevitable, result of earthly conditions?

Another explanation, often advanced by Europeans, is that American Christianity does not take sufficient account of the dark fact of sin. In this observation, also, there is doubtless some truth—a fact that American Christians themselves are beginning to recognize. Yet it is not true that American Christianity is wholly unrealistic in its view of man. There is, to be sure, an important difference between the European way and the American way of looking at man. The one is speculative, the other empirical. The one views man in the light of theological theories concerning his "nature," both before and after an alleged "fall" in the childhood of the race; the other takes account of observable attitudes and acts. But, leaving aside the question which of these two approaches is the more profound, it may at least be said for American Christianity that it has not been left entirely at the mercy of a facile and foolish optimism. In this country, also, Christians have some realization of the fact that the human heart can be desperately wicked. Indeed, not a few of them can supply specific and detailed information concerning man's inhumanity to man and his awful repudiation of God.

For my own part, I am driven to the conclusion that the most telling of all reasons why some Christians are pessimistic and others are optimistic as regards the future of the world is to be found in the fact that they hold quite different views of the activity of God in history.

All Christians, of course, reject the view that history is but a continuation of the biological process that operates in nature; that man is nothing more than an animal, "higher," it may be, than all other animals, yet not essentially different from them. All Christians reject the view that history is meaningless; that all man's hopes and efforts, all his struggle and pain, are but a phantasmagoria of fleeting appearances that have no significance whatever. With one accord, Christians reject the view of the ancient world, revived in our time by Nietzsche and Spengler, that history is but a futile cycle of birth and decay; that civilizations, like individuals, appear only to die and be buried; that there is, in fact, no future for the world save a tragic repetition of what has already been. Also, with one accord, Christians reject the view of Aristotle, and of some modern philosophies of the absolute, that what happens in history is of no concern to God; that God, indeed, is not even aware of what is going on in the world; that human laughter and human tears, the experience of individuals and the fate of nations, have simply no place in the consciousness of God. And all Christians reject the view that God's relation to history is only that of a spectator, who watches, it may be, with lively interest the successive moves of the game but himself takes no part in it. As all Christians see it, history is "the disclosure of spiritual reality"; it is shot through with meaning and significance; it is the theater of creative power, which brings into existence new conditions and values: not only above history but in it is God, who, indeed, is the only Actor who never disappears from the historic stage.

Up to this point there is universal agreement among Christians, all of whom believe that God is not only aware of man's predicament but concerned to do something about it. All Christians, however, do not hold the same view of God's activity in history. Some believe that God works in history to save individuals *from* the world, allowing the world for the most part to shift for itself. Others believe that God's concern for the salvation of individuals leads him to work, also, for the salvation of the world, that is, of political institutions, social customs, and economic practices. The first of these views is characteristic of European Christianity, especially on the continent, but it is by no means confined to Europe. The second, since the beginning of the present century, has become increasingly influential in American Christianity, but it is not simply an American development. It is now to be found, at least in some Christians, in almost every part of the world—a fact that came to light at Oxford in the summer of 1937 during a conference that included representatives of forty-three nations and 119 Christian communions. Hence, it cannot be said of these differing views of God's activity in history that they are but the product of different temperaments and conditions. It can be said of them that they are themselves productive of profound differences in human outlook, attitude, and conduct.

The first view makes for pessimism as regards the future of the world. God himself is not greatly concerned about the world; he is concerned only to deliver men from the toils of an earthly existence and to prepare them for entrance into that unseen world of the spirit where alone his kingdom is or ever can be. In the eyes of God, history is important only in so far as it provides a training ground for eternal life. Across the field of history pass the many generations of men, and as they pass God is not greatly concerned about the external conditions of their pilgrimage, whether there be freedom or bondage, justice or injustice, peace or war. Under any conditions, is not his grace sufficient to deliver the trusting soul from its earthly foes and to secure for it some blessed foretaste of eternal bliss? No doubt, the historic field is violently different from what it would have been if man had not sinned. With its revolting injustices, its sickening brutalities and occasional catastrophes, it is not as God meant it to be. It is what man has caused it to be. But not even God is now undertaking to transform it, his one great concern being, as has been said, to bring human beings safely out of a world such as this into a world that is unseen and eternal.

This view of God's activity in history is, to be sure, the traditional view—a fact which to some minds may suffice to commend it. Others, however, may become convinced that this traditional view is keeping Christians from seeing a number of things, which, *as Christians,* they really ought to see through the eyes of a profound concern. They may even begin to suspect that it is at least partly responsible for the historic fact that today, after nineteen centuries of Christian evangelization, vast numbers of human beings can find employment only in munition factories, where they are busily engaged in forging the instruments of their own destruction. In Europe, for centuries, Christians supposed that there was really nothing that they could do, or should even attempt to do, about the external order of the world; that God alone could transform the structure of society; and that he was not concerned to do it, his concern being only to attend and assist the individual soul in its passage "through time into eternity." Hence, they gave no thought, much less effort, to social reconstruction. They accepted the existing order of society, however saturated it might be with injustice, violence, and cruelty—seeking from time to time to curb its excesses but making no attempt to change and improve its essential character. Then, as conditions grew worse, they felt ever more bound to suppose that the victory of God must be achieved not in history but beyond history. A vicious circle in which unbelief in the possibility of social improvement consented to the development of situations that appeared to justify such unbelief.

Now, there must be something wrong with a view of God that leads men to believe that any attempt to correct outrageous conditions is not only futile but presumptuous. What *is* wrong with this traditional view of God's activity in history? Is it not the assumption, which underlies it, that the human soul is quite independent of its earthly environment? It is believed that God profoundly cares for the human soul. It is not believed that he is very much concerned about the social conditions in which the soul is placed; for it is assumed that social conditions of whatever kind can neither promote nor obstruct the soul's salvation. But is this true? It certainly is not true if what is meant by salvation is a spiritual condition that manifests itself in active good will toward men—all men—and in unswerving trust in God.

It is now generally recognized that the years of childhood are very important years. As is often said, they are the most impressionable years of man's life. Undoubtedly, they leave their mark upon us. Early "impressions" of whatever kind are not easily effaced. It must make some difference to the welfare of the soul if, in childhood, it is placed in a slum whose heroes are gangsters, or in a penthouse whose background is that of irresponsible wealth, or in a totalitarian state where "right" and "wrong" are considered to be but relative terms whose content is to be determined by the aims and requirements of national policy. And what of the soul of an adult? Is there no obstacle to a man's salvation in economic practices which forbid him to love his competitor as himself, or in a class system which stamps upon him the mental features of a lord or of a lackey, or in a political regime under which he is required to be cruel to persons of another race *or else* go to a concentration camp, which, considering that he has not only a soul to save but a family to support, the ordinary man is not likely to do?

If, as all Christians believe, God is profoundly concerned for the human soul, it cannot be that he is unconcerned about the social conditions in which the soul is placed. Hence, that other view of divine activity in history which holds that God's very concern for the salvation of individuals necessarily leads him to work, also, for the salvation of the world itself, those political institutions, social customs, and economic practices that so largely condition the spiritual development of men.

From this it does not follow that there are in the world unseen forces that are making automatically and inevitably for the improvement of society. It was once thought that men are bound to serve the common good, even though their designs and intentions are purely selfish. Adam Smith, the great political economist, argued that even the most rapacious of men are led by "an invisible hand" to bring about a just distribution of the product of human toil. Archbishop Whately reflected upon the wonder of a divine providence by which men are led to "render the greatest service to the public when they are thinking of nothing but their own gain." But now, certainly, we are in a position to affirm that no mysterious power transmutes the lead of human selfishness into the gold of human service.

Nor is there any "process of history" that is making inevitably for a condition of social justice, human brotherhood, enduring prosperity, and enduring peace. In Marxist theory, history is the product of a dialectical process in which one economic system, in the days of its apparent triumph, brings about conditions that give birth to its opposite, whereupon these opposed systems, in mortal combat, produce a situation in which the best features of both are preserved and united in a new system that is better than either of those it has superseded. Thus, communists believe that the capitalist state, triumphant in its power to produce but lacking power to distribute, has itself brought into existence the forces that are undermining it—at home, chronic unemployment and spreading want in the midst of potential plenty; abroad, ever more desperate, destructive, and inclusive wars. They believe that capitalist individualism, thanks to a one-sided and extreme development, has created the present demand for collectivism. They believe that the conflict between these contrary principles will eventually be resolved in a classless society that will include them both and which, with its civil liberties plus its co-operative practices, will be superior to any society the world has yet known. And this, they believe, *must* come to pass in consequence of the working of a dialectical process that achieves the reconciliation of contrary tendencies in a more inclusive society and which, in the long run, is irresistible.

This confident expectation is an act of faith, if ever there was one. And concerning this faith of communism, two things require to be said. One is that history may not always conform to a neat and logical pattern. In fact, it has not always conformed to this dialectical pattern. Capitalism, when it superseded feudalism, did not conserve the best in feudalism, which was its insistence upon mutual obligations. As Marx himself declared: "The bourgeoisie, whenever it got the upper hand, put an end to all feudal, patriarchal, idyllic relations, pitilessly tore asunder the motley feudal ties that bound man to his 'natural superiors,' and left remaining no other bond between man and man than naked self-interest and callous cash payment."[2] Is it yet certain that communism, as in Russia, will conserve the best in capitalism—as, for example, its civil liberties? True, Marxist theory does not suppose that the dialectical process is wholly mechanical. It assumes that this process operates through human wills and that it may, by them, be to some extent controlled and modified. Yet, according to Marxist

[2] *The Communist Manifesto,* 1918 Edition, pp. 27-28.

belief, human wills are themselves but the product of economic conditions, and one may surely question the realism of a faith that takes no account of such non-economic but ever-present factors as man's love of power and the awful blindness and cruelty which that engenders. As a description, however inadequate, of the activity of God in history this alleged dialectical process may be of value. As a substitute for God it has, I should think, a fairly big job on its hands!

To believe that God in history is seeking alike the redemption of the individual and the redemption of society is *not* to believe that the progress of civilization is inevitable. It *is* to believe that the issues of history are not merely in the hands of natural forces productive of climatic changes, nor merely in the hands of human forces such as the inventions of man's hands and the desires of his heart. It is to believe that the issues of history are finally in the hands of God, who transcends both nature and man. Given the Christian faith concerning the nature of God, it is to believe that the incalculably greatest of all forces now at work in the world is a power that is Christlike in character.

Now one can hardly hold this view of God's activity in history and oneself remain passive in the presence of outrageous conditions. The traditional view allowed comfortably sit uated Christians to *feel comfortable* in social conditions tha afforded *them* many delightful opportunities but which *fo the multitude of men* provided only a bare existence fraugl with insecurity, misery, and fear. How very different th view which forbids a Christian to remain at rest in a situ tion that spells loss for his neighbor even though it may sp gain for himself! *God* is not content with that situati *God* is attempting to correct it. And he is calling for vol teers to help him correct it. When it comes to the m tenance of a cosmic order, God requires no man's assista but when it comes to the achievement of a historic justice peace, he is necessarily dependent, to some extent, upor man co-operation. Hence, this view of God's activi history leaves the Christian with a goading conviction

confronted with a situation that is plunging millions of his fellows into a black abyss of misery and despair, he simply cannot look on and do nothing, *unless he is capable of deserting and betraying God.*

Attempting to do something, the Christian will need to maintain an attitude of profound humility in the presence of God, allowing him to reveal his plan of action. All too often, well-meaning men have supposed that their own idea of what ought to be done was, of course, God's idea of the true course of history. To how many participants in the World War did it ever occur that their own idea of Christ, in khaki, seeking with a bayonet to impose democracy and peace upon the world might be not a little abhorrent to God? Nor is this the only historic case in which, as we now have abundant reason to suppose, God's idea of what ought to be done was something quite different from the idea that well-meaning men had. Again and again, as Saint Paul observed, "God has chosen that which is foolish in the world to shame the wise; He has chosen what is mean and despised in the world—things which are not to put down things that are."[3] He has acted contrary to the expectations of reputed authorities, distinguished ecclesiastics, and professional reformers.

No doubt, we should be prepared to discover that some of the things we are eager to preserve—our own privileges, for example—are not the major concern of God; and that some of the things we are anxious to prevent, including, it may be, a more equitable distribution of material goods, are firmly imbedded in the purpose of God. We should be prepared to discover that God's way out for China, for Spain, for all of Europe, and, indeed, for all mankind, is something different from the way out that we conceive. It may even be discovered that God's purpose for the human race does not call for the preservation of "civilization" as we now know it, although one may confidently suppose that it calls for the preservation of the highest achievements of human culture and of methods and means of cultural achievement.

[3] I Corinthians 1: 27, 28. (Moffatt's translation.)

A clear view of God's activity in history is certainly conducive to a sense of humility. It is *not* conducive to a sense of dismay. After all, it is God who is concerned for the improvement of the world, not merely a handful of human idealists; and God, although he does of necessity employ human agents in the field of history, is by no means wholly dependent upon the insight and effort of men.

It is God, not man, who creates and maintains a cosmic order in which human existence is possible.

It is God, not man, who provides natural resources, over which nations now fight like dogs over a bone, but which surely might become, as they no doubt were intended to be, the necessary foundation of an all-inclusive world culture.

It is God, not man, who is responsible for a moral order in the nature of things which places limits upon the power of men to do evil in the world. The existence of a moral order which no nation nor civilization can successfully defy is at once the insight of religion and the experience of history. The individual, it is true, may do evil and get away with it. He may spread himself like a green bay tree, acquiring riches, prestige, and power. When his brief day on earth is over, he may die comfortably in bed at peace with himself, and the local press may make out that he was but little lower than the angels. The fact, however, requires to be noted that under modern conditions even the evil-doing individual may be unable entirely to escape the social consequences of his acts. In a closely knit and high-powered civilization, such as we now have, the time-span between economic cause and economic effect is far shorter than it once was, so that the economic freebooter, although he may still die in his bed, may not die either with his worldly possessions or with his worldly reputation completely intact.

But let that be as it may. What greatly concerns us is the undeniable fact that evil institutions, evil customs and practices, encounter at last a moral order which leaves them in the condition of a jerry-built house after a Kansas cyclone. In the fourth century, the peoples of the West, including

Christians, could not believe that their society was going to pieces, weakened though it was by many internal and external strains, any more than we can believe that our society is in process of dissolution. But this, at least, history has made abundantly clear: no society that countenances greed, injustice, violence, and cruelty can permanently endure. And it does look as if God were saying to our generation, "You had better mend your ways; you had better start building a co-operative society in which as individuals and as nations you can work together for the common good of all." The "stars in their courses" do fight against evil, and it is God, not man, who has created them.

It is God, moreover, who is ultimately responsible for the conversion of men. It is the Hound of Heaven who tracks men down and brings them to their senses. It is the Light of the World who opens men's eyes to saving truth, so that they, in turn, bring light to their fellows. The world-embracing vision that is now the possession of growing numbers of men; the insight into world conditions, why they are as they are; whole-hearted devotion to the world's improvement and the very faith which supports such devotion—all this is a result of God's activity in history. It is he who has profoundly helped to bring about these human achievements of vision, of understanding, of Christlike devotion—of which, almost certainly, there are more to be found in our time than in any period of the past. And it remains to be seen what God can do with such human instrumentalities as are now presented to him by enlightened and determined minorities.

This view of God's activity in history knows no despair. It cannot abide a defeatist spirit. Holding this view, the Christian can believe with Isaiah that in the hands of God "the nations are as a drop of a bucket"; he can ask with Saint Paul, "If God be for us, who can be against us?"; he can look straight at the worst in the world of today and be fortified to know that the future of mankind is in the hands of God, not in the hands of proud and selfish men.

CHAPTER II

THE KINGDOM OF GOD

Where, then, are we to look for the kingdom of God? Not on earth alone.

There is something repugnant in the idea of a historical process that, like a juggernaut, rolls over a thousand generations of men *only* to the end that there may be, at the last, an enraptured generation enjoying the blessings of liberty, justice, and peace. It is not that in preceding generations men are asked to labor for goods that they themselves will never know; the best of men are glad of a chance to do that. It is rather that in preceding generations so many men are placed in conditions that offer them little or no opportunity to become the best of men. Not only are they denied any chance of happiness; they are denied any chance of development, being stuck in the mud of a situation that is at once brutal and brutalizing. Are they, then, merely the biological means of a process that, caring nothing for them, is only concerned with some eventual achievement of good in history? That is an idea that fits quite snugly into the philosophy of fascism, which has no compunction about sacrificing the individual for the sake of national power or of racial glory. It is, however, wholly incompatible with the Christian view of God and man.

On earth, moreover, history is destined probably to come to an end. A world without an atmosphere, as uninhabitable as the moon—such is the fate that scientists foresee for the little planet that now supports us. Nor do they consider it probable that human life is now to be found on any other planet. Summarizing the views of present-day science, a recent writer concludes: "It is clear . . . that life hangs by a thread in the universe, and that of the nine known worlds only on the Earth and Mars are physical and chemical conditions such that life is possible. And Mars is a shriveling, senile world, dying for lack of water. The probability is strong that intelligent life is absent. A little scrubby vegetation alone may remain to testify to what the planet may once have been—something as eloquent as the Maya ruins of Yucatan. . . . Can it be that a thousand million stars were created in order to produce a planetary cinder or two with just the right conditions for the support of life?"[1] To which one may well add the question, "Can it be that human life is destined eventually to disappear from the earth and leave no trace behind?" What is here involved is not merely the fate of individuals, whether they are to be preserved or not. Also involved is the fate of truth, right, and love, to preserve which the best of men are prepared to suffer the loss of all things, but which would not be preserved but would themselves be blotted out if all conscious life should be destroyed.

If the kingdom of God is only to be found on earth, there is no escape from pessimism as regards the ultimate future of mankind and all for which at their best men care and hope and strive. It is, however, the Christian faith that the kingdom of God is not to be found only on earth, or on some other planet that likewise, in time, may become uninhabitable.

> The body they may kill:
> God's truth abideth still,
> His kingdom is forever.

Furthermore, the kingdom of God, as Christianity conceives it, stands for a reality that transcends any possible achievement on earth. It stands for the rule of God over every domain of human life—a rule not externally imposed but inwardly accepted by men and women who, seeing in God what Jesus saw, feel bound and glad to fulfil "the first and great" commandment: "Thou shalt love the Lord thy God with all thy heart and with all thy soul and with all thy

---

[1] Waldemar Kaempffert: article in *The New York Times Magazine*, July 31, 1938.

mind"; and "the second," also, which is "like unto" the first: "Thou shalt love thy neighbor as thyself."[2] Is such a reality possible under earthly conditions of time and space? It certainly is not easy for a Christian in America to love his neighbor in China as himself. Nor is this only because of the political situation that now obtains in the world. It is also because at a distance of some six or eight or even ten thousand miles he cannot know, except in the most general of ways, what his neighbor's needs are and how, therefore, he may serve him. Space does present a formidable obstacle to the realization of the Christian ideal for human relations. And what of time—those so few years that are given us on earth to master the claimant demands of the flesh and to learn what life is really about? Does even the most saintly of men, as he approaches the end of the earthly pilgrimage, feel that he has faithfully and fully met every demand of love? And what of every new generation that comes into existence? Even a classless society would have to reckon with the fact that "every new generation is a fresh invasion of savages"—a fact that may not be conceded by the "fresh savages" themselves, especially in this country, but which will hardly be disputed by parents, schoolmasters, or traffic cops. Hence, it can hardly be supposed that a society fulfilling every condition and demand of love toward God and man will ever appear on earth.

Yet Christian faith, which holds that the kingdom of God, in all the truth and beauty of its perfection, will never be realized on earth, may also believe that even on earth men should hope and strive for an endless approximation to it. And this, growing numbers of Christians are now convinced, Christian faith must believe and require. To be sure, we have here no "continuing city," as the New Testament reminds us and modern science flatly informs us. But surely it does not follow that we should permit such cities as we do have to become and remain corrupt. Granted that earth can never be heaven, it hardly follows that we should allow it to

---

[2] Matthew 22: 37-39.

become hell. A Christianity that specializes in an other-worldliness that is quite unrelated to this world's affairs has something in common with a dictatorship whose search for trouble abroad is nicely calculated to divert attention from trouble at home. It has, however, but little in common with the New Testament. A Christianity that, being convinced that the ideal is too high for earth, does not promote but rather discourages any attempt to improve earthly conditions greatly needs to be viewed in the light of the saying of the Lord: "After this manner pray ye: Thy kingdom come, Thy will be done in earth as it is in heaven." That saying, according to any possible interpretation of it, does not support the view that this tormented planet can never witness anything other or better than the existing state of the world.

Human finiteness and human sin do indeed place limits upon what is possible in history. They forbid the hope that the kingdom of God may ever fully come on earth. They do not, however, compel the conclusion that this world is bound to have political conditions in which men are denied every kind of freedom, or social conditions in which some are given the privileges of lords and others the duties of lackeys, or economic conditions in which despairing multitudes are left "ill-fed, ill-clad, ill-housed," and permanently unemployed. Neither human finiteness nor human sin forbids the hope of vastly better conditions in a world where *God* is seeking alike the salvation of individuals and the salvation of society.

Of course, Christian prayer for the coming of God's kingdom on earth is primarily an appeal to God, not to men, to do something about the world. The contrary assumption, that it is primarily an appeal to men, has turned out to be a tragic mistake, as not a few earnest Christians in recent years have discovered. They were eager to do something in the way of the world's improvement. They set out with the best of intentions and no serious misgivings. They devoted themselves to good causes. They did not bother to inquire into the will of God for the world, partly because they were too busy and partly because, as they tacitly assumed, they already knew it! In fact, without intending to do so, they very nearly lost sight of God. Then, when their own efforts failed, they felt completely let down; nor could they find comfort in the fact that some of their devotion, as they felt bound to admit, had been ill-conceived. The "social gospel," contrary to the oft-repeated assertion of its opponents, did not fail to see that the task of world improvement is a two-handed job, calling for the transformation of individuals as well as for the reconstruction of the social order. But the social gospel, in all too many cases, did leave people with the impression that the task of world improvement was primarily their own; which is also to say that it finally left them disillusioned, painfully confused, and not a little dismayed. This tough task of world improvement is far too big for men to tackle alone. It becomes for men a possible task only when they keep their eyes on God, realizing that he it is who must see it through; and that, as for themselves, they can hope to be effective only if they seek, in utter dependence on God, to discover and promote his idea of a good world.

But how are we to know what is God's idea of a good world? The New Testament, it must be confessed, offers nothing in the way of concrete suggestion for the improvement of society. It has no social program. This, I say, requires to be confessed; but it does not require to be lamented. The early Christians, including the writers of the New Testament, were children of their time, as are all the sons of men. Had they endeavored to formulate a political or economic program, they inevitably would have been influenced by existing practices and opinions; and the result, in view of the enormous prestige which the New Testament was destined to acquire, might have been disastrous. They might, for example, have given formal approval to the institution of slavery, which in the ancient world was taken for granted. Moreover, the social requirements of men, like train schedules and weather reports, are subject to change. A single invention such as the automobile may create new social demands. In the horse-and-buggy age, traffic signals and motor cops were unneeded. But try without them to get around in any big city today. In an industrial civilization, economic practices that developed under agricultural conditions are found to be hopelessly inadequate. It is not, therefore, to be lamented that the New Testament contains no blueprints of the City of God. No generation of Christians—not even our own!—may hope to devise plans for the construction of society that will be valid for all time. There is and can be no political state, no economic system that may claim to represent the only pattern that is compatible with the mind of Christ.

Are we left, then, without any clue to the will of God for our age in respect of the social order? Assuming that the will of God for any age will be relevant to the peculiar conditions of that age, are we bound to suppose that there is in God's will for the world nothing that is universal, nothing that is timeless, and nothing, therefore, of which we may ever be sure? As Christians, how can we come to that conclusion? Do we not believe that the true nature of God has been made manifest in history in the person of Christ? And are we not bound, therefore, to suppose that the will of God for any age, whatever it may comprise, will be steadfastly Christlike in its aims and mandates? Negatively, we may be very sure that the will of God calls for nothing that is cruel or unkind. Positively, we may be equally sure that what it does call for is the very utmost which, in a given historical situation, a Christlike love is able to achieve. To be sure, concrete solutions for concrete problems will always remain to be discovered; and not even Christians can dispense with intelligence. But this is by no means to say that Christians can but blindly grope in their search for some clue to the will of God for their day and generation. They have the surest of all clues in the face of Jesus Christ.

Thus, as regards human relations, Christians may be quite certain that God does not approve of cruel discriminations based upon racial prejudice. An early Christian, born a Jew, who thought all Gentiles were beyond the pale of heaven's concern, was granted a vision in which it was made clear to him that God "has no favorites, but he who reverences Him and lives a good life in any nation is welcomed by Him."[3] Moreover, the God of Christian faith desires and seeks to effect the highest possible development of every son of man; which is also to say that he wholly deplores any social condition that prevents or impedes personal development. Christians may be very sure that anti-Semitism is an "abomination" unto God. They may be equally sure that God "abhors" the way in which Negroes are treated in most communities in the United States, including colleges and universities into which a few of them are somewhat grudgingly admitted. At this point, the undergraduate reader may stop long enough to reflect upon the social situation that obtains on his own campus. Does he know of any "Christian" Greek-letter fraternity that has ever invited a Jewish student to join it? Are Negro students permitted to use the swimming pool? If so, under what conditions?

It is, no doubt, a significant fact that racial prejudice does not appear in young children. Little Gentiles, their parents being willing, get along very well with little Hebrews. In some cases, little white boys play happily with little black boys until frightened mothers tell them they mustn't do so any more. Racial prejudice is not instinctive; it is acquired. It is a social, not a biological, inheritance. Children are not born prejudiced; they have prejudice thrust upon them. Prejudice, moreover, cannot be defended by the assertion that there are, after all, fundamental differences between races. There is no ground for such an assertion. All the races of men can interbreed. (Most of them have done so.) All races can and do produce superior individuals. Roland Hayes, a pure-blooded Negro, has absorbed the best in Anglo-Saxon culture. The mentality of cultivated Asiatics is certainly as distinguished as is that of cultivated Europeans. And neither Europe nor the United States can point to any

[3] Acts 10: 34, 35. (Moffatt's translation.)

living son who in spiritual stature rises higher than a son of India whose name is Gandhi or than a son of Japan whose name is Kagawa. Nor has science as yet furnished any indisputable proof that there are races that, inherently, are "superior" or "inferior." Today, judged by the best in Anglo-Saxon culture, the Negro, undeniably, is a backward man; just as, twenty centuries ago, Angles and Saxons, judged by the best in Greco-Roman culture, were backward men. But in the evolution of a race a thousand years are but as yesterday when it is past, and who can say what the relative position of human groups will be a few centuries hence?

Certainly, every human individual has a right to be judged by his intellectual and spiritual attainments and not to be discriminated against because of his race or color. "What I demand," said Count Okuma, "amounts to this: That the present racial standards shall be replaced by the standards of civilization." To be refused admission to a hospital when one is critically ill, to be excluded from hotels, restaurants, theaters, and bathing beaches, not because one is an uncultivated person but merely because one is a colored person; to be despised, snubbed, and excluded for no reason at all except the fact that one belongs to a race that has produced Isaiah, Spinoza, and Einstein—such is the present fate of many a high-grade and sensitive person in a world that is torn by prejudices that are as irrational as they are cruel.

Finding their clue in the face of Jesus Christ, Christians may now surely conclude that they are called of God to eradicate racial prejudice from their own hearts and unceasingly to strive for its removal from their society, in order that a time may come when no man, because of his race or color, shall be denied opportunity for personal development and achievement or be refused the respect to which, by reason of his personal attainments, he is undoubtedly entitled.

As regards the economic order, Christians may be quite certain that God does not approve of such gross inequalities of economic condition as may now be found in nearly every country in the world. In the United States, a report recently published by the National Resources Commission indicates that during the year 1935-36 the poorest third of American families and individuals received no more of the total national income than was received by the richest one-half of one per cent. It is true that this measurement was made before income taxes were deducted. Nevertheless, as *The New York Times,* after taking account of every mitigating fact, feels bound to admit: "The contrasts in income to which this report calls attention are really shocking."[4] In 1930, two million American farmers received no more (gross) for all the wheat and cotton they produced than was the total income, in 1929, of 513 supremely wealthy individuals.[5]

What is here at stake is, of course, nothing less than the spiritual development of men; for material possessions of some amount and kind are an essential condition of all the higher activities of the human spirit. Almost any student now enrolled in an American university could easily give the names of other young men and women whose intellectual capacity is undoubtedly as great as his own, but who, for financial reasons, are denied the opportunity of a college education. Consider, also, a few quotations from a recent report to the American Youth Commission of the American Council on Education: "Forty per cent of employable youth have been unable to find work"; "Among the most favored class of employed youth sixteen to twenty-four years of age—those in cities—the median wage is generally in the neighborhood of twenty-five dollars a week. The proportion of youth who work without wages is surprisingly large"; "One-eighth of first admissions to state (psycopathic) hospitals alone in 1933 were between the ages of fifteen and twenty-four"; "The depression forced some one and a half million young pepole who normally could have been married to postpone this step." To the few, gross inequality of economic condition brings terrible temptation to adopt false standards of human worth, to

---

[4] Editorial, *The New York Times,* September 4, 1938.

[5] Lundberg, Frederick, *America's Sixty Families,* Vanguard Press, p. 410. $3.75.

spend fantastically, and to live irresponsibly. To the many, it denies or at least limits opportunity for decent housing and decent surroundings, for adequate medical and dental care, for education, and even (periodically) for employment.

Also, Christians may be quite sure that God does not approve of a staggering concentration of economic power in the hands of a few individuals. After exhaustive research, Berle and Means express the amply supported judgment that half of industry in the United States is controlled and directed by approximately two thousand individuals out of a population of 125 million. They add: "The recognition that industry has come to be dominated by these economic autocrats must bring with it a realization of the hollowness of the familiar statement that economic enterprise in America is a matter of individual initiative. To the thousand or so men in control, there is room for such initiative. For the tens and even hundreds of thousands of workers and of owners in a single enterprise, individual initiative no longer exists."[6] Nor does this control of industry stop with industry. It affects business, even big business. It exerts a powerful influence over newspapers. Its influence over government is tremendous. Such concentration of power is undoubtedly dangerous. It may result in financial panics, in economic depressions, and in international wars. In fact, it has done so. Moreover, as Professor John Bennett points out in the first volume of the HAZEN BOOKS ON RELIGION, "This concentration of power makes most people afraid—afraid to lose their jobs, to speak their convictions, to let it be known how they vote, to antagonize the powers that be in the community for fear of losing customers or clients or the sources of institutional incomes."[7] (Similar fear may be felt on a college campus where a very few students are in a position to control elections and social life.) Excessive economic power, no less

[6] Berle, Adolph, and Means, G. C., *The Modern Corporation and Private Property*, Macmillan, pp. 32-125. $3.75.

[7] A free quotation from *Christianity—and Our World*, Association Press, p. 38. 50c.

than excessive political power, is bound to be spiritually disastrous both for those who wield it and for those over whom it is wielded, producing in the one case the attitude of the autocrat, in the other the attitude of the yes-man.

Equally obvious is the judgment of God upon an organization of society that, being fiercely competitive, inevitably makes for friction and conflict between individuals, classes, and nations. As I have elsewhere said: In a competitive world, where men selfishly, recklessly pursue private gain; where, indeed, with such economic weapons as tariffs and currencies, they fight one another for the possession of wealth, prestige, and power—in such a world there is bound to be war and preparation for war, for there is bound to be injustice, resentment, and fear of reprisal. In such a world armaments are but the outward, visible sign of an inner strife.[8]

Human attitude toward material possessions is, of course, not wholly determined by the economic order in which people live. In any "order" or "system" men may develop that love of money that has been declared to be the root of all evil. It may, however, be said that modern society, to an extraordinary degree, has fostered the belief that material possessions are "the supreme object of human endeavor and the final criterion of human success"—a belief that must be repugnant to God.

Finding their clue in the face of Jesus Christ, Christians may now surely conclude that the economic order which they are called of God to create would do at least these four things: (1) It would see to it that opportunity for the development of personality, such as material goods may provide, was distributed as widely as possible. (2) Leaving adequate room for individual initiative, it would none the less hold economic power strictly accountable and place it under some kind of social control. (3) It would enable the whole economic process, by which man gets his daily bread, to partake more and more of the character of a great co-operative under-

[8] Tittle, E. F., *A Way to Life*, Holt, p. 49. $1.75.

taking making for the common good of all. (4) By no means indifferent to material goods, it would make it possible for the minds of men to be far more free than they now are to give attention to the goods of the spirit.

The physical limits of this small volume do not permit of the concreteness which at this point is greatly needed. I only may say that Christians, in my judgment, should now undertake, through political organization and action, to achieve the objectives indicated above, and they also should take an active part in the formation of co-operative societies, both of consumers and of producers.

Need Christians today feel wholly in the dark concerning God's will for the political state? Of the state, a Russian writer, whom the Archbishop of York has pronounced one of the great writers of our time, has this to say: "The state regards as permissible all that serves its preservation, expansion, and power. It is utterly impossible to apply to the state the same moral standards as to an individual. Actions considered evil, immoral, and deserving of condemnation in an individual are regarded in the case of the state not merely as permissible but as fine and noble. It is, apparently, impossible to require that the state should obey the Ten Commandments; they are only applicable to individuals. Individuals are forbidden to kill, and murder is considered a great sin. But the same individuals acting on behalf of the state as its organs and instruments not only may but must kill, and so far from being regarded as a sin it is considered their duty."[9] Now, there is one part of this statement that Christians, as all other persons now alive in the world, are bound to accept; the part, that is, that describes the existing situation. Today, there is hardly a state on earth which, from the Christian standpoint, is not in much of its conduct as immoral as a Sicilian bandit. But what of the other part of this statement, which flatly says that it is

---

[9] Berdyaev, Nicholas, *The Destiny of Man,* Scribner, p. 253. $5.00. Elsewhere, in this same book, the author does not hesitate to predict that war will be destroyed.

utterly impossible to apply to the conduct of the state the same moral standards which are now applied to the conduct of individuals? Can Christians accept that? I do not, myself, see how they possibly can.

It is, of course, true that large bodies of human beings are much more difficult to handle than are individuals. There is the awful drag of custom, of ignorance, and of inertia. There is the dreadful susceptibility of the mass mind to irrational fears and prejudices. Yet the state, after all, is no superhuman being. It is not a god, nor an angel, nor a devil, nor a blonde and buxom maiden in a Wagnerian opera. If it were not for the presence of human beings, the state would have no existence. The state is the people who compose it, nothing less and nothing more. It has no body apart from their bodies, no mind apart from their minds, and, of course, no conscience apart from their consciences. Politics, as also economics, is not a self-governing force quite independent of the thoughts, desires, and practices of human beings. From this it follows that the state may do any number of immoral things; it is, indeed, almost certain to do them if the people who compose the state are willing that they should be done—willing, that is, to elect or to tolerate political leaders who are capable of doing them. But should Christians be content with that kind of political leadership? Should they even by their silence contribute to a public sentiment that is prepared to acquiesce in national conduct that is shockingly different from decent individual conduct? Should Christians themselves be prepared to act differently in public office than they would feel bound to act in private life, adopting in the one case moral standards strangely at variance with those which they recognize in the other? In this connection one may recall the Scotch Calvinistic divine who, holding forth vigorously on the wrath and sure punishments of God, felt bound apologetically to explain: "You know, the Almighty has to do some things in His official capacity that He would scorn to do as a private individual!" But, looking into the face of Christ, one can hardly suppose that God is prepared to acquiesce in a moral dualism which not only permits a nation to sin against other nations, but also permits an individual to sin against his neighbor, provided only that he does it in some official capacity. Nor can one suppose that human consent to such moral dualism will lead in the long run to anything save disaster. Failure to apply the Ten Commandments to the conduct of nations has led in our time to a World War, the Treaty of Versailles, the Smoot-Hawley tariff, the re-armament of Germany, the rape of Ethiopia, horror in Spain, the invasion of China, the unsettlement of Europe, the insecurity of the world. It certainly does not now appear that the welfare of the national state calls for theft, murder, false witness, and covetousness.

What is God's will for the state? What it will finally call for I, for one, do not pretend to know. But, assuming that the clue to it may be found in the face of Christ, Christians, I should think, might well suppose that it now makes at least three important demands.

1. It calls for a state in which government rests, at last, upon the consent of the governed; for the reason that absolute power never can be safely intrusted to any man or group of men. Whether it be aristocratic or theocratic, plutocratic or proletarian, dictatorial power is bound to be a menace to the welfare of individuals and the welfare of the world.

2. It calls for a state that will provide for its members such all-essential conditions of personal development as freedom of conscience, free access to facts, freedom of teaching, and freedom of discussion. It is not enough that the state should provide employment, important though that is; or that it should raise the material level of life; or that it should cause public officials to be efficient, city streets to be cleaned, and scheduled trains to run on time. All these are good, but they are not enough. Nothing is enough which stops short of conditions in which the human soul has a fair chance to thrive.

3. It calls for a state that will place itself under the same law of service that is held to apply to individuals and which,

in obedience to that law, will consider itself bound to serve not only its own people but all mankind. The fascist state, as its spokesmen never weary of informing us, has given its people something to live for besides money-making—a national good and glory in devotion to which even the humblest of individuals may find his life stripped of drabness and clothed in the splendor of a heroic purpose; and this, they insist, is in marked contrast to the democratic state, which is content merely to exist, to provide jobs for perennial office seekers, and to maintain economic conditions in which a very uncertain number of persons may secure feathers for their own nest. In this contention there may be some truth—more, indeed, than we of "the great democracies" are willing to admit. But the fact remains that the fascist state is at once enslaving the minds of its own people and threatening the security, the prosperity, and the culture of every other people on earth. What is called for by the will of God is a state with a mission in the world so truly great and so inclusive that not only may its own people, in the strength of it, be lifted up, but all men may find themselves in conditions affording greater security and greater opportunity.

Does this, although inspiring to think about, seem quite beyond the reach of human effort? Yes, not only does it seem to be, it *is* quite beyond the reach of human effort. But is it beyond the reach of God's effort? Long ago a Man who suffered death on a cross had a vision of the future of mankind whose brightness far exceeded the brightness of any vision that is ever likely to come to one of us. Did he suppose that what he saw was something too wonderful for even God to bring to pass? No; and Christians, if they are in the least worthy to bear his name, will not now allow themselves to act on any different conclusion.

CHAPTER III

THE CHRISTIAN REVOLUTION

Revolutions of the classical type are seldom if ever revolutionary. True, they bring about change of one kind or another; but the change, of whatever kind, is rarely fundamental. Power changes hands. There is a new set of masters. But the new masters, after but a brief experience of power, reveal in themselves a striking likeness to the old, being jealous of their authority, brooking no opposition, suppressing the slightest nod of dissent. Wealth, also, changes hands. There is a new set of moneyed men, who, after but a brief experience of affluence, exhibit a marked resemblance to previous possessors of riches. The nobility give way to the bourgeoisie, who soon develop much the same characteristics as appeared in the class they superseded. The royal autocrat gives way to the tribune of the people, who presently thinks, feels, and acts very much like a royal autocrat. The capitalist gives way to the proletarian, who, when he gets hold of a little money, begins to think, feel, and act very much like a capitalist. Before long, many of the evils in the old order that the revolution pulled down reappear in the new order which it has set up. There has been much change but little progress, much suffering but little gain. Such gain as there has been is shockingly disproportionate to the amount and kind of loss which the revolution has entailed.

Now, Christianity certainly aims to be revolutionary. What it contemplates is nothing less than changed men in a changed world; and the change, in both cases, is expected to be fundamental. What is more, Christianity *is* revolutionary. Of certain early Christians it was said, "These that have turned the world upside down have come hither also."[1] And this, although it was said in condemnation, was truly

[1] Acts 17: 6.

said. That is precisely what genuine Christianity is concerned to do and may be expected to do whenever it is let loose in the world. The powers that be, in so far as they are selfish, are always afraid of genuine Christianity, and with abundant reason. They have no fear of corrupted Christianity, which, as they soon discover, they are easily able to control and even to utilize to their own advantage. But of genuine Christianity they stand in unholy awe. Here is something that they are unable to control and that is ever seeking to control them. Here is a power that, given time and even half a chance, may be expected to unseat selfish power, as every tyrant knows.

Early Christianity accepted the Roman state, but it did so in a fashion all its own. Its adherents did not conspire against the emperor, however cruel and corrupt he might be. They merely ignored him, until they were bidden to worship him; then they defied him. "Christianity, in spite of all its submissiveness, did destroy the Roman state by alienating souls from its ideals. It has a disintegrating effect upon all undiluted nationalism and upon every form of exclusively earthly authority."[2] If only early Christianity had itself remained uncorrupted, would the history of Europe have been mercifully delivered from many of the chapters it now contains? Would the condition of mankind have been far different and vastly more promising than it is today? This much, at least, may confidently be said: Whenever Christianity has been released in the world, it has brought about fundamental changes in human hearts and in human relations. In some parts of the world, thanks to Christianity, there is today, on the part of growing numbers of men, a new attitude toward women, a new attitude toward children, and a new attitude toward the "forgotten man."

From revolutions of the classical type, Christianity differs in three all-important respects. It differs in respect of the values that it recognizes and seeks to promote. It differs in

---

[2] Troeltsch, Ernst, *The Social Teaching of the Christian Churches*, Macmillan, Vol. I, p. 82. $10.50.

respect of the importance it attaches to the need of change not only in the external arrangements of society but also in the hearts of men. It radically differs in respect of the means which it employs to achieve its ends.

I

As regards the values it recognizes, Christianity is nothing if not revolutionary. "Lay not up for yourselves treasures upon the earth, where moth and rust corrupt and thieves break through and steal; but lay up for yourselves treasures in heaven, where neither moth nor rust doth corrupt and where thieves do not break through and steal."[3] That certainly is revolutionary. Treasures in heaven or treasures on earth, which do men commonly prefer? Which do they regard as the more important? Is it not commonly assumed by the critics of the existing order of society, hardly less than by the defenders, that treasures on earth are "the supreme object of human endeavor and the final criterion of human success"? Whereas Christianity, which by no means despises daily bread but recognizes the need of it and even urges men to pray for it, insists that the supreme object of man's quest is not bread but God, and that the final criterion of his success is the judgment of God—that and nothing else.

"Ye know that the princes of the Gentiles exercise dominion over them, and they that are great exercise authority over them. But it shall not be so among you: but whosoever will be great among you, let him be your minister; and whosoever will be first among you, let him be your servant: even as the Son of man came not to be ministered unto, but to minister, and give his life a ransom for many."[4] That certainly is revolutionary. That is radically different from the conception of greatness that now prevails among men. One may venture to suppose that this Christian view of greatness is now held by a much larger number of persons than it was nineteen centuries back; but considering not only the rulers

[3] Matthew 6: 19-20.
[4] Matthew 20: 25-28.

of nations, the captains of industry, and the field marshalls of finance but also the princes of the church, one can hardly suppose that even today this Christian view of greatness is the common understanding of the world. The ordinary man, whether he be a defender or a critic of the existing order of society, does not assume that the meaning of greatness is some unusual capacity matched with a consuming desire to be a servant of mankind. As defender of the existing order, the ordinary man is far more likely to think of greatness in terms of power to control the lives of others. As critic of the existing order, he is not unlikely to think of it in much the same fashion, the issue between him and the defender being not so much over the meaning of greatness as over how much opportunity there is in the existing situation to achieve the kind of greatness which both desire. The defender is content with the existing order, seeing that it offers him all the opportunity he could hope for to realize his dream of power. The critic is discontent with it because he sees in it no chance to realize *his* dream of power. Not always but all too often, the flaming radical is, at heart, a frustrated reactionary. Hence, given power, he quickly sheds every garment of radicalism he has ever worn and appears in a new suit of precisely the same cloth and cut as that worn by men whom he has bitterly assailed. British Toryism, which understands this sufficiently well, has thus far succeeded in taming nearly every lion that stood in its way. It has given him at least the appearance of such power and glory as he craved and, lo! he has become as tractable as a lamb.

Christianity, which urges men to seek first not wealth or power but the kingdom of God, is undoubtedly revolutionary. It also is wise. Seeking first wealth or power, what do men get? It now appears that what they get is a world war, followed by a world-wide economic debacle, followed by insane preparation for another world war, which, if it comes, may usher in another dark age. It now appears that what they get is hell on earth. Surely, living men have reason to suppose that if you seek first economic goods, not to mention social prestige and power, then other goods—such as liberty, justice, security, peace, and decent human relations—will not be added unto you but will, on the contrary, be taken away from you. Christianity is at once revolutionary and right in saying, "Seek first the kingdom of God and such economic goods as are really essential to human life and development will be given you."

II

Christianity further differs from classical revolutions in respect of the importance it attaches to the need of change in the human heart. At this point there is certainly a difference in emphasis. For the classical revolutionist, although he may assume the need of some change in human motivation, does not suppose that a new heart is the primary condition of radical social reform; whereas the Christian revolutionist insists that without it radical social reform is impossible. The former holds that a transformation of human desire and purpose, although no doubt helpful, is not essential, at least not at the start. The latter holds that even at the start it is all-essential to success, if what is meant by success is something new and something better. Concretely, the classical revolutionist believes that the leaders of a revolution need not themselves be dependably just or merciful or unselfish or kind. The Christian revolutionist believes that a revolution, unless its leaders are dependably just, merciful, unselfish, and kind, will lead but to some new form of tyranny and oppression.

There is also a difference in what is expected from improved social conditions. The classical revolutionist believes that, given improved social conditions, you can confidently expect improved men and women; you can expect people to think, feel, and act quite differently than they did before. The Christian revolutionist believes that, given improved social conditions, you can thank God that human nature, at long last, is being accorded a better chance to develop its latent possibilities of good; but he is very far from believing that improved social conditions will automatically produce better men and women.

Now, in the light of the contemporary situation it can, I think, hardly be denied that of these two kinds of radicalism the Christian is by far the more profound. Indeed, as compared with Christian radicalism, the more common variety would seem to represent the dream world of an inexperienced child. The real world is not such that good ends can be achieved in it by men who themselves are not good. Nor is it such that, given only some improvement in social conditions, one may reasonably expect a corresponding improvement in human lives, as anybody ought to know who knows anything about the inner life of a university or of a favorably conditioned suburban community.

There is here, however, no ground for complacency on the part of Christians, not even on the part of evangelical Christians who have insisted all along that what is needed is a new mind, a new heart. For the kind of new man that evangelical Christianity, for the most part, even now envisages is not a kind that may be expected to help much in the building of a better world. Some years ago, at a convocation held in memory of a beloved teacher, I delivered a brief address in which, among other things, I said of this teacher that he had put to shame the cynicism that maintains that human beings cannot be expected to put forth their best efforts unless there is held before them, as a carrot before the nose of a donkey, the hope of some great material reward. Shortly afterward I received from a prominent churchman a letter that said, "It is hard for me as a practical man to see any analogy between the motives which actuate a college professor, a teacher, or a missionary and the motives which, perforce, must actuate a man who engages in business in a responsible way." What a pitiful confession of spiritual blindness! Yet in fairness to the man who unwittingly made this confession, it should be remembered that evangelical Christianity had allowed him to suppose that he *was* the possessor of a new mind, a new heart. Was he not "true" to his wife, a man of "character" and "integrity," in short, a "model citizen"? Did he not support the church and various educational and philanthropic enterprises? What more was required of him? Evangelical Christianity had allowed him to suppose that nothing more was required of him, although by his own admission he was actuated by motives which he would have considered discreditable in a missionary, a clergyman, or a teacher—motives that have led men, although with no deliberate intention, to do things that have terribly contributed to the present chaos in the world.

Unlike classical revolutions, the Christian revolution first calls for a new kind of man—a man so truly new, so radically different, that, in whatever station he is now or ever may be placed, he can be depended upon to seek first not his own material or social advantage but that ideal society for which the kingdom of God magnificently stands.

III

A third difference between the Christian revolution and classical revolutions has to do with the means it employs to reach the ends it is seeking to achieve.

As everyone knows, classical revolutions do not hesitate to make use of the means of violence. There is street fighting in which people are killed. There is a forcible seizure of power. Then there are deliberate executions. Anyone whose continued existence constitutes a threat to the new order is summarily put out of the way. Then there is likely to be a counter-revolution, which, if it occurs, proves to be as savage as it is desperate. Moreover, the mere threat of a counter-revolution may lead to the systematic "liquidation" of whole groups and classes of persons. Then steps are taken to insure the success of the revolution. A dictatorship is established under which freedom of every kind is suppressed. All means of communication, including the press and the radio, are placed under a rigid censorship. Every agency of instruction, also, is placed under state control. A spy system is created to inspire fear and compliance. And woe unto anyone who does not avoid even the appearance of dissent! All this, at least at the start, is, of course, well intentioned. It is thought to be necessary and, therefore, to be justifiable. It is expected to clear away the debris of an old order and to open up the way to a new order in which methods of coercion will no longer be needed. Yet, as has been said, it is now a notorious fact that classical revolutions are seldom if ever revolutionary. There is, it may be, some gain; but there is also terrible loss. After the passage of many years, the world, essentially, is found to be much the same as it was before.

What is the explanation of this bitter defeat of good intentions, high hopes, and heroic efforts? Two reasons we have already advanced: no revaluation of values, no adequate concern for the transformation of the individual life. And a third, I should think, is now apparent; namely, the means that the classical revolutionist has employed.

1. The means of violence are inherently unsuited to the achievement of any good end. Always and inevitably, violence is productive of hate, lies, coercion, fear, and consuming desire for revenge. Can love be born of hate? Can truth be established by lies? Or freedom by coercion? Can a good and stable civilization emerge out of cold fear and hot desire for revenge? Antecedently, it does seem unlikely. In the light of history, it should now be considered impossible. Concerning the present situation in the Soviet Union, Professor John Dewey, who will hardly be accused of extreme conservatism, has recently said: "The vicious element in the whole (Marxist) conception is that the end is so important that it justifies the use of any means. . . . In fact, however, it is the means employed that decide the ends or consequences that are actually attained."[5]

At this point it requires to be said that every argument against a violent revolution is, under present conditions, an argument equally valid against international war fought

[5] Article in *The Washington Post,* December 19, 1937.

in hope of achieving some laudable end. A war to end war and to make the world safe for democracy, or, as it is now being said, a war to stop dictators and to check the advance of a militaristic fascism—a war to achieve any good end is, of course, in the same category as a revolution to prepare the way to Utopia. War, which *is* violence used on an enormous scale and quite indiscriminately, cannot now possibly lead to any good end: for it now involves not simply a small professional army but vast populations; it now calls for the deliberate killing not only of men but of women and children; it now demands a deliberate, systematic, and wanton manufacture of lies; it now calls for a dictatorship that immediately denies every kind of freedom and eventually threatens the recovery of freedom; it now destroys not only wealth but the process by which wealth is produced; and, what is much more, it now tears to pieces the whole body of law, order, and decent habitual practice which centuries have been required to produce and without which civilized life simply cannot survive. War under present conditions is itself so inherently evil and so certainly, inevitably productive of evil that it cannot possibly lead to any good end. On the contrary, it is bound to lead to the very opposite of what those who engage in it, provided they are decent men, sincerely and even passionately desire.

2. Also, the means of violence are grotesquely unsuited to human nature. Man is an animal who sometimes is stupid, often is vain, and always is inclined to be selfish. Yet he is, after all, a rational animal who can be reasoned with, provided you go about it in the right way. Contemporary opinion to the contrary has largely resulted from attempts to reason with people in the wrong way. Advocates of pacific means of settling disputes have urged malcontents to refrain from war and passively to accept a situation that was favorable enough to the advocates but definitely unfavorable to those whom they were seeking to persuade. In that situation, the malcontents, it must be confessed, have stubbornly refused to be persuaded; whereupon the advocates have decided

that they were wholly unreasonable, they could not be made to listen to reason, the only language they were capable of understanding was the bark of a big gun.

This breath-taking leap to the conclusion that you must be incapable of listening to reason if you will not agree, without violent protest, to let me keep what I have, no matter how much it is or how I came by it, brings up another fact about man; namely, that he is a sinner: a fact which Americans today are quite willing to admit as regards Japanese; and Britons, also, as regards Germans, Italians, and "lesser breeds without the law." Thus, a distinguished English churchman, speaking of armaments, feels constrained to say: "It is useless for the sheep to pass resolutions in favor of vegetarianism while the wolf remains of a different opinion." Which sounds not a little clever and convincing. But is it, after all? It would, perhaps, be completely convincing if only Great Britain or France or the United States *were* a sheep wholly innocent of any desire to claim and possess the lion's share of the world's territory, markets, and raw materials. It cannot, however, be wholly convincing in clear view of the fact that the sheep itself, in this case, is not exactly a lily-white animal in which there is no guile. If we may venture to suppose that this English churchman had his own government in mind when he thought of sheep passing resolutions in favor of vegetarianism, we may properly remind ourselves that his own government, during recent months, has not wholly refrained from wolfish conduct such as the bombing of helpless women and children on the northwest frontier of India. It is, indeed, useless for the sheep to pass resolutions that it does not itself fully intend to respect. And as for a sheep that is attempting to make off with nearly everything in sight, it no doubt should provide itself with a motorized army, a mighty navy, and an overwhelming air force! Even then it may feel the need of "collective security."

The use of violence involves two assumptions. One is that I am rational but you are not. The other is that you are a sinner but I am not. The fact is that you (a German?) are too rational to give an everlasting assent to conditions that are themselves irrational and unjust. The fact is that I (an Englishman? an American?) am myself too sinful to be able to use violence against you redemptively.

3. Finally, the means of violence are tragically incompatible with the nature and purpose of God. For the nature of God is love and the purpose of God calls for the development of human beings who will freely choose what is true, right, and good. Such, at least, is the Christian faith, which today, whether in the presence of science or in the presence of history, has no occasion to feel apologetic. Need it be said, then, that God cannot be expected to approve of means of social improvement that require persons to treat other persons as though they were not persons but only inanimate objects to be bombed out of the way? Need it be said that God cannot be expected to bless or countenance a social process that seeks to compel men to do what the human initiators of it think they ought to do and are determined they shall do or die? And need it be said that means of social improvement which are utterly incompatible with the nature and purpose of God cannot possibly achieve any good end?

Now, it is undeniably a fact that Christians, as all other persons, are members of a society whose economic practices in many cases involve the use or threat of violence. The United States Senate Committee on Civil Liberties has brought to light the sinister fact that certain American industries, in their attempt to prevent the organization of labor, have employed spies, inspired brutal attacks upon organizers engaged in lawful activities, and met lawful picketing with clubs, guns, and gas. Hence, some Christians argue that, being themselves the beneficiaries of an economic situation that appears to involve the continuous threat and frequent use of violence, they have no moral right to protest against the employment of violence by people who are seeking only justice for themselves and for others. It may, however, be doubted that this is a tenable position. Christians, of course, have no moral right to acquiesce in injustice; they are morally bound to condemn it and to do all they can to correct it. But surely they are not bound, in their attempt to correct it, to use methods that seem to them to be unwise, unchristian, and ultimately ineffectual.

There is today a growing number of Christians who consider themselves morally bound to reject the means of violence and to employ only such means of social change as are compatible with the ends they are seeking to achieve, as also with the limitations of human nature and with the nature and purpose of God. As they see it, the Christian revolution must commit itself to a social process that relies upon education and political action. The education, of course, must be radical in the sense that it undertakes to enlighten men's minds and to transform their hearts so that they will desire and seek the common good. The political action, also, must be radical in the sense that it undertakes to change and improve the external conditions in which men are required to live and labor. Thus, political action, under Christian influence, would seek within the nation to initiate an economic process that would lead to an equitable distribution of economic goods and opportunities. Also, it would seek, through international conferences, to bring about a new state of world affairs in which no nation would insist upon being judged in its own cause, no nation would claim or covet individual ownership of undeveloped territories, and no nation would seek monopolistic control of markets and raw materials, but all nations would find it to their own advantage to respect economic agreements that are just and to settle by peaceful means any dispute between them.

A social process of this character is likely to be slow in its redemptive operation. But is there any short cut to a good world? And is it necessary that revolutionaries, before they die, should be able to rejoice in the triumph of their undertaking? Is it not enough that they should have some personal part in a redemptive process that will go on after they die and which, in the hands of God, will eventually secure the triumph of *His* undertaking? Long ago, the Greatest of

Revolutionaries was taken up into a high mountain and shown all the kingdoms of the world and the glory of them and told that he might have them if only he would use the devil's means to get them. He did not close with the offer. He chose, instead, the way of the cross. And is it not a fact that in *that* way of sacrificial appeal to the minds and hearts of men, leading to new habits of thought and practice, has come the only real and enduring progress the world has known? Christians might well venture to suppose that the way of the cross is God's way of redemption; that God, had there been a less costly or a more rapid way, would have found and used it; that there is, when all is said, *no other way*.

CHAPTER IV

CHRISTIANS AND THE WORLD

Christians have always lived in an unchristian society. The present is by no means the first time in history when the social order, viewed from the standpoint of the New Testament, has appeared, in many of its aspects, to be atheistical and immoral. In the first century, an earnest Christian, observing the social scene, felt constrained to say, "The whole world lieth in darkness." To an enlightened Christian conscience, much of the world, from that day to this, has appeared to be very dark indeed. War, it hardly needs to be said, is no new thing under the sun, nor is grinding poverty, nor callous cruelty, nor exploitation in its most naked and shameless form. One may venture to suppose that the attractiveness of the monastic life, during the Dark Ages, was due to not only religious aspiration and a desire for holiness, but also to a less pious desire for physical and economic security. Men fled from the world at once to escape sin and to escape the rigors and terrors of secular life. In the thirteenth century, the medieval Church, at the height of her power, claimed the whole of human life as her parish, asserted her freedom from secular interference, issued orders to kings, merchants, and money-lenders, and gave to Europe more, probably, of law and order than it ever had before or ever has had since. Yet even in that astonishing century there were cruelties of a kind that many modern stomachs would find nauseating; of which not a few, it must be confessed, were perpetrated by the Church herself. Alleged heretics were sometimes punished not so much because of their "heresy" as because of their property, which the Church coveted and confiscated for the financing of a magnificent and costly institutionalism. As a land owner, moreover, the Church was no more just or gentle than the commonality of land owners in her treatment of tenants and serfs. Not every bishop who lost his head at the hands of an outraged peasantry was a suitable candidate for the martyr's crown. In the thirteenth century, the Church became a civilization; but Christendom, judged by the mind of Christ, has never been Christian.

What attitude have Christians taken toward political institutions, social customs, and economic practices which, at best, have been sub-Christian and which, at their worst, have been scandalously anti-Christian? They have taken, it appears, no less than six attitudes. (1) They have been indifferent to a world which they believed to be passing away, looking for another world soon to come direct and pure from the hands of God and faithfully preparing themselves to receive it. (2) They have fled from the world into some "retreat" where, in monastic seclusion and discipline, they have sought at once inner peace in this life and eternal bliss in the next. (3) They have conceived and asserted the right of religion to rule over the whole domain of human existence. At the same time, however, they have accepted the existing order of society, attempting only to curb the worst of its excesses. (4) They have passively accepted the external conditions in which their lives were placed, believing that the world's inequalities and brutalities are at once the result and the punishment of sin, that human effort is powerless to remove them, that God alone can do anything about them. (5) They have established a religious community, on a voluntary basis, in which they have undertaken to actualize, in every field and in every relation, the Christian ideal of love. (6) They have not only affirmed the relevance of the Christian faith and the Christian ethic to every aspect of man's life on earth but, also, they have resolutely undertaken to secure for "the mind of Christ" a noble embodiment in the institutions of society. Christians have, indeed, reacted in different ways to their earthly environment; and these various reactions, most of which are of long standing, may now be appraised in the light of their historic effects.

I

The early Christians took no interest in the "world." As they saw it, love of the world was at once sinful and foolish, inasmuch as the world was not only damned but doomed. Its days were numbered, and the end might come at any moment. Even as late as the first quarter of the fourth century, an expectant Christian could write: "The men famous for goodness before Moses lived when human life was just beginning and organizing itself. We live when it is near its end. They, therefore, were anxious for the increase of their descendants, and that the race might grow and flourish. But these things are of very little interest to us, who believe the world to be perishing and running down and nearing its last end . . . while a new creation and the birth of another age is foretold at no distant time."[1] Moreover, the idea of social progress through human effort was nonexistent in the ancient world. The Christian looked forward to a blessed future, but he did not suppose that the "holy city" of his dreams would be built by human hands. It would "come down from God out of heaven."

Nevertheless, the early Christians attempted to actualize in their own relations one to another the Christian ideal of love. "The multitude of them that believed were of one heart and of one soul; neither said any of them that ought of the things which he possessed was his own; but they had all things common. . . . Neither was there any among them that lacked: for as many as were possessors of lands and houses sold them, and brought the prices of the things that were sold and laid them down at the apostles' feet: and distribution was made unto each man according as he had need."[2] This, of course, was not modern communism, either in theory or in practice. Innocent of any kind of economic theory, it was a voluntary and, indeed, a spontaneous sharing of earthly possessions. Moreover, it did not involve "the public owner-

---

[1] Quoted from Eusebius by Inge, W. R., in *Christian Ethics and Modern Problems,* Putnam, p. 129. $3.00.

[2] Acts 4: 32-34.

ship of the means of production"; it was confined to the consumption of goods. But it was none the less splendid and significant. What a revelation of the instinctive action of the spirit of Christ! Here we may see how the spirit of Christ acts before it "adapts" itself to a given situation, makes "necessary" compromises with its environment, discovers ways of rationalizing its surrenders, and ceases to be the spirit of Christ. The New Testament, it is true, knows of no other experiment such as that which was tried in Jerusalem; but in the post-apostolic period, before Christianity had become thoroughly institutionalized, it was by no means uncommon for Christians, during periods of economic stress, to share with their fellows their earthly possessions, holding back nothing which love called for in the presence of need.

Nor was this spontaneous sharing of material goods the only expression in human relations of the spirit of Christ. There was no attempt to do away with the institution of slavery: God would attend to that, and soon, for the existing order of society was nearing its end. But the early Christians robbed slavery of much of its sting by treating the slave as a brother.

There were some things, moreover, that Christians, at whatever cost to themselves, would not permit themselves to do. They refused to participate in brutal games or to have any part, even as a spectator, in licentious drama. They refused to hold any office or to engage in any trade that might require them, however indirectly, to participate in idol worship or in the worship of the emperor or in the taking of human life—a refusal which in some cases was, no doubt, as difficult and dangerous as would, today, be a refusal in time of war to engage in any enterprise that was connected with military operations. Did Christians, in those days, refuse military service? Not all, but some of them did. Writing in the middle of the third century, Origen declares, "We do not serve as soldiers of the emperor even though he requires it." Tertullian (pp. 160-230) took the position that a converted soldier should leave the army if he could or, if he could not, he should suffer martyrdom; and there were Christians in the army who did suffer martyrdom rather than remain in a situation which they felt to be wholly incompatible with their religious faith.[3]

Early Christians, despite the fact that they had no thought of social reform, found themselves constrained by the love of Christ to do a number of things that had social consequences. Their actions often, if not their intentions, were revolutionary. They could not but obey the impulses of love to try and improve human relations at least within the circle in which they themselves moved. Unemasculated Christianity, under whatever social theory it may operate, cannot look upon suffering or injustice and do nothing about it. Yet it is now quite clear that the early Christian expectation of a near end to this present world was illusory. It is equally clear that the social outlook which this expectation produced is not one which modern Christians can afford to cultivate.

II

Monasticism, both early and medieval, was often an attempt to overcome the world by "abandoning" it. The monk had little or no thought of social improvement; his driving concern was an individual transcendence of earthly conditions. Incidentally, it is true, monasticism at its best rendered an inestimable service during those dark centuries that followed the collapse of imperial Rome. Monastic orders of the Benedictine type revived agriculture, taught useful arts, provided poor relief, treasured priceless manuscripts and produced and circulated elementary textbooks. Also, some of their members achieved a life of rare piety and loving1kindness, which, no doubt, exerted a cleansing, healing influence in an age that was notoriously brutal, turbulent and corrupt; and the fervent prayers of righteous men availed much. But the fact remains that the monk's

[3] See Cadoux, C. J., *The Early Christian Attitude to War,* The Swarthmore Press Ltd. $2.00.

motivation was largely egoistic. His primary object was to save his own soul; and he commonly thought of salvation in terms of escape from the torments of hell and of enjoyment of the rewards of heaven. In the hierarchal scheme of Thomas Aquinas, the monk's piety and virtue are the final triumph of a society whose lay members must of necessity make costly compromises with the world; but the social value that is thus attributed to monasticism represents, after all, a somewhat desperate, although sincere, attempt to justify a *fait accompli.* The monk *had fled from* the world.

What, then, may be said of monasticism? I fully agree with Walter Marshall Horton that "there is a great need in our day for modern religious orders living in a state of voluntary poverty and gaining by the manner of their life the right to speak with freedom and utter frankness to all parties in the contemporary conflict."[4] This, however, is not the kind of monasticism we now have before us; it has much more in common with the religious community idea, which we shall consider farther on. As for monasticism as it has commonly appeared in history, I can only say that in my judgment it leaves very much to be desired. Celibacy, no doubt, is a heroic achievement. Yet the discipline needed by the monk may be no more severe nor more persistent than is the discipline needed by the husband, assuming that each desires to be a Christian. Chastity in celibacy may not be a more difficult achievement than is gentle and intelligent unselfishness in marriage. As for cold courage, that which is demanded of the monk is not to be compared to that which is demanded of the merchant, assuming again that each desires to be a Christian. As a matter of fact, historic monasticism has quite as much of moral lapse in it and even of moral (and mental) abnormality as it has of high spiritual achievement. "Those who seek God in isolation from their fellowmen, unless trebly armed for the perils of the quest, are apt to find, not God, but a devil, whose countenance

[4] See Horton, W. M., *Realistic Theology,* Harper, p. 182. $2.00.

bears an embarrassing resemblance to their own."[5] In monasticism, after all, there is often something selfish which from the start militates against full attainment of that "mind of Christ" which led Jesus of Nazareth in love's name to fellowship with publicans and sinners. There is also an inevitable parasitism that eventually proves its undoing. The monk lives under the protection and, often, at the expense of a world he has chosen to ignore—a world that, sooner or later, obtains an unplanned revenge, if not in chaotic conditions threatening the security even of cloistered monks, at least in financial contributions to monastic orders that greatly reduce their chance of any free play of the mind, any untrammeled quest of the spirit.

In the twentieth century, at least in Protestant countries, monasticism is hardly what William James would call a "live issue"! Are we sure about that? Given another world war and such social disintegration as would inevitably follow it, the idea of a monastic "retreat" might make no slight appeal even to minds unsteeped in the Catholic tradition. Moreover, there is today a monasticism whose habitat is not a cloister but a classroom. A kind of secularized monasticism that permits of delights unknown to cowled monks (of the better sort), but which, after all, bears a certain resemblance to its medieval prototype, inasmuch as it chooses to remain aloof from the human struggle, seeking for itself the bright refinements of a "civilized" existence, content to derive its support from a world of business that it affects to despise, but which in the end calls the tune to which it dances. Monasticism, after all, may not be a dead issue.

III

A third attitude toward the world appears in medieval Catholicism, at least in its scholars and statesmen. Here, for the first time in history, the right of religion to reign over

[5] See Tawney, R. H., *Religion and the Rise of Capitalism,* Harcourt, Brace, p. 229. $3.50.

the whole life of man on earth is magnificently conceived and boldly affirmed. Medieval Christianity, as represented in a Gregory VII or in a Thomas Aquinas, would have been amazed at the idea that religion is purely an affair of the inner life, having no connection with political or economic activity. That a baptized lord might shamefully mistreat the serfs on his estate the medieval mind was prepared to believe; it would, however, have been shocked at the suggestion that such a man might, nevertheless, be beautifully Christian in his inner life. In the thirteenth century, the gospel injunction, "Beware of covetousness," was not understood to apply only to that portion of the day when a Christian is not engaged in economic activity. Unhappily for his peace of mind, it never occurred to the medieval merchant that if only he should beware of covetousness on Sundays he would be meeting the full requirement of God. Nor was the medieval business man permitted by the Church into which he was born to follow merely the dictates of his own conscience when he offered his wares to the public. The Church herself, in all cases where it seemed practicable to do so, attempted to regulate prices, in the belief that, as Saint Antonio put it, "to leave the prices of goods at the discretion of the sellers is to give rein to the cupidity which always goads almost all of them to seek excessive gain." The Church, moreover, had plenty to say concerning the practice of "usury," of speculation, of manipulating the market. Persons guilty of such practices were not only condemned but punished by ecclesiastical authority.

Medieval Catholicism, which maintained that economic conduct, like all other conduct, must be judged and governed by Christian standards, was equally insistent upon the relevance of the Christian ethic to political conduct. To the medieval mind, lay as well as clerical, the modern idea that the state is a law unto itself would have been shocking, if not wholly incomprehensible. There was, it is true, no little conflict between Emperor and Pope, not to mention lesser lights, over concrete questions of authority and administration; but both, in principle, were prepared to believe that the will of God is the ultimate standard of all human institutions and activities. The state, ideally conceived as the guarantor of law and order and as the protector of the weak against the cupidity of the strong, has, no doubt, an important place in the purpose of God. In this sense, "the powers that be are ordained of God." But if the head of the state derives his authority from God, it by no means follows, in medieval thought, that he is entitled to an unconditional obedience. Only so long as the emperor seeks to do the will of God by promoting the welfare of his subjects are his subjects under any obligation to give him their obedience. Otherwise, they are morally free and bound to obey God rather than man.

Thus, in the Middle Ages, the lordship of religion over the whole domain of human life was grandly conceived and asserted. Yet in all this there was no thought of radical social reform. The Church more or less complacently accepted the existing order of society. As has been shown, earnest attempts were made to regulate all human activity in accordance with the supposed demands of the Christian ideal. But these attempts, so far as Catholic officialdom was concerned, were made always within the framework of the existing order of society, which itself was taken for granted. Yet it was not a framework in which human life had a fair chance to make the most and best of itself. In theory, feudalism was a patriarchal system that embodied the principle of mutual obligations. If the peasant was bound to serve and obey his lord, the lord was equally bound to protect his villeins and to give thought to their temporal welfare. Theoretically, indeed, all the ranks of society, from the lowest to the highest, were bound together by reciprocal ties of loyalty and service. But there was, to put it mildly, a considerable variance between theory and practice. In reality, feudalism hardly resembled that idyllic picture that romantic imagination, undisturbed by historic fact, has so often drawn of it. In reality, it reduced multitudes of human beings to a permanent condition of serfdom in which they were bound to the land they tilled, were obliged to share the stables of the cows and sheep they tended, and were subject to the demands, however unreasonable, of their masters. In reality, feudalism was a system in which the few were enabled to profit by the exploitation of the many—a system that inevitably made at the top for pride, arrogance, and brutality, as it certainly made at the bottom for a coarse and degrading servility. But the Church accepted it without serious question. It might, as Saint Thomas believed, be the result of sin, a social condition due to man's fallen estate. In any case, it was supposed to be inevitable and immutable. Hence, during all the Middle Ages, except in the case of a few outlawed minorities, there was no serious thought of radical social reconstruction.

The effect upon the Church herself of this complacent acceptance of an unchristian order of society is surely deserving of note. The Church herself became ever more enmeshed in the toils of a system whose glaring abuses she sought to correct but whose fundamental incompatibility with her own ideal she chose to ignore. Thanks to numerous bequests over vast stretches of years, the Church found herself the greatest land owner in Europe. As such she became the possessor of multitudes of serfs—human beings—who came with the land they occupied, along with its houses and herds. Did an abbot, a bishop, or even an archbishop who thus became the lord and master of serfs find it easy to fulfill the law of Christ: "Thou shalt love thy neighbor as thyself"? On the contrary, he found it impossible. An order that stood for such vicious extremes as the position of a lord who might live by the sweat of other men's faces and the position of a serf who had no control over his own person or fortune was not an order in which love of one's neighbor could become a reality. As a matter of fact, the Church, as landlord, repeatedly violated ethical demands of whose validity, from her own standpoint, she could have no doubt. She even became involved in those private wars between land owners, which she undertook to prevent only "from Thursday to Monday and in certain holy seasons of the year."

The feudal order, without theory or design, emerged in Europe during the chaotic period that followed the breaking up of the Roman Empire, when hungry and imperiled individuals were glad to attach themselves to some securely established land owner and become his man in return for his protection. But it lingered on for centuries after any real occasion for it had ceased to exist; and the medieval Church, by accepting and rationalizing it, became herself so infected with its spirit, its false standards of value, its absurd pretensions, its greed and injustice and cruelty, that her voice, at the dawn of the sixteenth century, had ceased to make any Christlike appeal to the conscience of mankind. It is, apparently, not enough for Christians to concern themselves with the "typical" abuses of a social order that in itself is incompatible with the mind of Christ.

IV

Another attitude toward the world appears in Lutheranism and, more often perhaps than not, in modern evangelicalism. Luther himself had no doubt of the sovereign right of religion to rule over the whole domain of human life. Despite his disaffection toward the Roman Church, he was far too good a Catholic for that. In his view, the world of business was by no means either below or above moral law and religious sovereignty. "A man should not say, 'I will sell my wares as dear as I can or please,' but, 'I will sell my wares as it is right and proper.' For thy selling should not be a work that is within thy own power or will, without all law and limit, as though thou wert a god, bounden to no one. But because thy selling is a work that thou performest to thy neighbor, it should be restrained within such law and conscience that thou mayest practice it without harm or injury to him."[6] A pronouncement that is hardly equivalent to the modern assertion that "business is business."

But Luther (was it because of his experience as a monk?) had a strong distaste for ecclesiastical regimentation in daily life. There was, he contended, no need for the Church to tell her sons what was right and what was wrong in political or in economic conduct. The Christian's own conscience, instructed by God speaking directly through the Bible, could be counted upon to do that. (A belief whose naïveté is equalled only by its variance with the hard facts of history.) Luther, moreover, who had little, if any, confidence in the princes of the Church, had, it would seem, an amazing confidence in the princes of the state. Secular authority, he thought, could be depended upon to act as a strong servant of God in the political and economic spheres. Hence, Christians could well afford to leave all political and economic questions with their earthly rulers! In any case, there was nothing they could do about their social environment. The institutions of society—State, Mart, Court, Constabulary, Soldiery—were willed by God in the interest of man's temporal welfare. He it was who created them "as he did the moon and other creatures." They all, no doubt, have become more or less corrupt in consequence of human sin. Still, God permits them to exist just as they are, with all their corruptions, either because, bad as they are, they are not ill-adapted to man's fallen estate or because, being bad, they are a befitting punishment for his sin, a suitable rod for his correction. And only God can change them. Only he who willed (or permits) them can redeem them. Any attempt on the part of Christians to improve them would be not only futile but presumptuous.

Hence, in Lutheranism, religion tends to become divorced from all secular interests and activities—an affair almost purely of the inner life. There is, to be sure, wistful hope that the personal piety of true Christians will at least to

[6] See Luther's *Works*.

some extent illuminate the darkness and heal the hurt of the world. But there is no idea of any obligation resting upon Christians to labor for the world's redemption. Theirs but to respond to divine grace and to proclaim its wondrous availability to all the sons of men; the rest belongs to God. Thus a modern Lutheran does not hesitate to say: "The word of God which the Church preaches is directed to the community of Jesus Christ; i. e., to every individual human being in so far as it calls him into that community, not, however, to the social structures which organize and maintain this world."[7]

Nor is this position now to be found only in Lutheranism. It appears in many a churchman who believes that Christianity is solely concerned with the individual and his private relations to other individuals; who indignantly repudiates the suggestion that it has something to say about business and industry, politics and diplomacy.

What happens when Christians take this attitude toward the world? Mischief! If it does not start, it eventually appears in Christians themselves. Luther, it should be remembered, did not suppose that the Christian's spiritual life is something apart from his economic activity. He supposed that a true Christian would reveal his spirituality in the ethical quality of his conduct in the world of affairs. But such complete separation of the Church from the world as Lutheranism called for led, however illogically, to the conclusion that spirituality is quite unrelated to political and economic conduct. It is the fruit of theological belief and religious emotion, not of daily attitudes and acts. It has nothing to do with earthly struggle but only with otherworldly visions, hopes, and assurances. "Spiritual exercises" are confined to such practices as "devotional reading" and prayer and worship; they do not involve any nobly peculiar kind of activity in the world of business, politics, and

[7] Werner Wiesner, in *Christian Faith and the Common Life,* Willett, Clark, p. 102. $2.00.

finance. Hence, the all-too-typical churchman of today whose difference from the unchurched multitude lies largely in the fact that he goes to church and contributes to its financial support, not in any radical departure from current habits of thought and conduct in the social group to which he belongs. Christianity *may* become secularized in the hands of Christians who, ignoring its religious faith, attempt to apply its ethical principles to the institutional practices of the world; it *has become* secularized in the hands of Christians who, denying its relevance to the institutional practices of the world, have themselves become, in nine-tenths of their living, undistinguishable from worldlings.

Behold, also, how great a mischief this attitude produces in the institutions of society. Left to its own devices, the secular world pays less and less attention to the claims of religion and the demands of personal morality. It bitterly resents any attempt on the part of the Church even so much as to pass judgment upon its standards and practices. It develops its own laws, which bear striking resemblance to the laws of the jungle. It even creates its own gods—Material Success, Social Prestige, National Power. It runs amuck, fighting and killing in the name of its gods. It becomes unbalanced, mentally and economically, with resultant strains and depressions. An overweening desire for material gain, unchecked by any religious or ethical consideration, produces its own punishment. A situation develops in which producers cannot sell because consumers, having been denied a fair share of the earnings of industry, cannot buy. Under ruthless competition the economic field becomes a battlefield in which men fight, first with tariffs and quotas, finally with guns and gas.

All this, of course, is very far from the intention and expectation of Luther, who naïvely supposed that it was quite safe, in the economic sphere, to let each man follow his own conscience, and that all matters touching man's temporal welfare could be safely intrusted to secular authority. Yet this position of Luther has involved for the world a condition of anarchy such as it has hardly known since the close of the Dark Ages, and it has involved for the Church a condition of social impotence in the face of mounting disaster. In Germany, today, a church which, for four hundred years, has been content to leave the world in the hands of the state finds itself compelled to fight for its very existence against the totalitarian claims of a state that has ruthlessly invaded even that "spiritual" realm—theological doctrine and religious instruction—which has so long been regarded as the sole, but indisputable, domain of the Church. It is only fair to add that the Confessional Church in Germany is now making explicit what certainly was implicit in Luther's own position. The Barmen Synod has issued a statement that says: "We repudiate the false doctrine that there are spheres of our life in which we have not to recognize Jesus Christ, but another Lord, spheres of life in which we have no need of justification and sanctification through Him." Grand indeed is the heroism of many a Christian in Nazi Germany, who, in the face of the known horrors of the concentration camp, is refusing to deny his faith. Even now, however, as regards the political and economic spheres, the historic position of German Lutheranism remains unchanged. The Christian, in so far as his own conduct is concerned, is bound in these spheres also to "recognize Jesus Christ"; he is not bound in Christ's name to undertake any kind of radical social reconstruction.

V

We have next to consider the attempt of minority groups, both Catholic and Protestant, to achieve on a small scale and on a voluntary basis a community life that would be in harmony with the Christian ideal.[8] Such an attempt was made in the twelfth century by the Waldensians; in the fif-

[8] For a much fuller treatment, see Troeltsch, Ernst, *The Social Teaching of the Christian Churches,* Macmillan. To this magnificent work I am greatly indebted, as anyone is now bound to be who enters the field it exhaustively covers.

teenth century, by the Taborites and the Moravian Brethren; in the sixteenth century, by the Anabaptists and the Mennonites; in the seventeenth century, by the Levelers and the Diggers. These adventures, for the most part, were initiated by people who belonged economically to the "lower orders" of society, and it is fair, perhaps, to suppose that their economic condition had something to do with their desire for a "holy experiment" in Christian living. Something, but not everything. In many cases, certainly, there was an impelling sense of moral outrage at the way in which official Christianity had compromised with the world, and a goading desire to live day by day in blessed harmony with the teachings of Christ. The communities that were thus established by these discontented folk varied, of course, one from another. But in most cases they were organized on a democratic basis; they forbade their members to "take an oath," to "go to court," to "accept usury," to bear arms, or in any way to use force or violence; they sought to prevent the appearance of social divisions and classes, requiring all their members to live simply and unostentatiously; they encouraged the development of such virtues as honesty and chastity, humility, forgiveness, generosity, and kindness; they undertook to embody the radical ideal of the Sermon on the Mount.

Such an attempt deserves to succeed. There is something grand about it, as a later age, never the contemporary one, always feels. But does it succeed? Indirectly, no doubt, it accomplishes no little good. It disturbs the conscience of official Christianity, whose representatives first try to stamp it out, then (second generation) assume toward it an attitude of cool and superior indifference; but finally (later generations) use it in sermonic efforts as an illustration of Christian faith and daring! Yet not only does it fail radically to transform the world, which it hardly hoped to do; it fails after a time to be the source of any fresh stream of thought and action.

Some of these radical Christian communities did not manage to last very long; they were extirpated by a world that refused to stand for such "dangerous nonsense." Others have lingered on, but at terrible cost; for their members, fearful of the world's contamination, have refused to participate even in its culture. They have become a "peculiar people," but hardly in a sense which Saint Paul would have appreciated; their "zeal" finding expression in somewhat petty eccentricities, so that they are noted today not so much for their refusal to sin as for their refusal to shave and to wear buttons.

It is, apparently, impossible to live in complete detachment from the world, except at the price of cultural disintegration and intellectual sterility. Even the Moravian Brethren, as they increased and prospered, found it necessary to do business with the world, often on the world's own terms. Intelligently conducted religious communities, both because of their superior morale and because of their practice of co-operation, are likely to prosper in a material way. Consider the Mormons, how they thrive. As they prosper, they are forced more and more to have dealings with the outside world and thus to come under its influence. Christians cannot get away from the world, and unless they undertake to change the world into the image of Christ, the world is likely to change them into its own image.

Having said this, I am, none the less, prepared to believe that there is still need of voluntary associations of men and women who will make yet once again a heroic attempt to live at once in the world and above the world. As Aldous Huxley has said, "Most people find example more convincing than argument. The fact that a theory has actually worked is a better recommendation for its soundness than any amount of ingenious dialectic."[9] There is still need for experiment in communal living on the basis of a common religious faith, a voluntary sharing of material goods, and a resolute commitment to the use of non-violent means of social reform.

---

[9] Huxley, Aldous, *Ends and Means,* Harper, p. 147. $3.50.

VI

Calvinism, it appears, must be given the credit, if credit is due, for having inspired and carried out the first attempt in history to Christianize the whole social order. This statement, however, needs qualification; for the "Christianity" which Calvinism undertook to embody in social institutions was derived quite as much from the legalism of the Old Testament as it was from the teaching and spirit of the New. Everything was regulated—the rate of interest and grace before meals; the price of meat and the time that might be devoted to "honest" games; the fee to be charged for a surgical operation and the hour (9 P. M.) for innkeepers to put their guests to bed. Regulations, of whatever kind, were strictly enforced. Any attempt to disregard the enactments of the Consistory was almost certain to be discovered—there were spies in every corner—and the punishment meted out, even for trivial violations, was likely to be severe. Not only murder and adultery but blasphemy and heresy were punishable with death. And the charge of heresy was almost certain to be brought against anyone who was rash enough to criticize the regime. To obtain "confessions," torture of the most revolting kind was systematically employed. All things considered, it is safe to assume that Jesus Christ, had he appeared in Calvin's Geneva, would have wanted it understood that he himself was not a "Christian." It is also safe to assume that he would have been tried for heresy and sentenced to be burnt, as Servetus was, with slow fire.

Theocracy is of all dictatorships the most terrible. Never is absolute power so ruthlessly exercised as it is in the hands of a man who honestly believes that he is giving voice and effect to the will of God, as John Calvin and Adolph Hitler have made abundantly clear. It may certainly be said that a Christian society, assuming that it is possible, will never appear in the form of a theocracy. It is simply unthinkable that a Christian society could ever be established by such methods as theocrats are always tempted, and always consent, to employ. Theocracy, moreover, with its tacit assumption of infallibility, develops in the theocrat a megalomania that blinds his eyes to what is involved in the Christian view of the world.

The attitude, however, that we have now under consideration does not necessarily lead to Calvin's Geneva. An attempt to "Christianize" the social order may be quite differently conceived. It is today being conceived in a radically different fashion by growing numbers of Christians. They differ from early Christianity both in their belief as to the duration of this present world and in their assumption that human effort to improve the social order is by no means bound to be wholly ineffective. They differ from some forms of monasticism in their belief that it is cowardly and unchristian to flee from the world in quest of a private salvation. They differ from medieval Catholicism in their refusal to assume that the existing order of society is, from the Christian standpoint, good enough or that it is, in any event, unalterable. They differ from Lutheranism, as from other similar positions, in their rejection of the idea that Christian responsibility ends with the bare proclamation of the Gospel. They differ from religious "communalism" in their inability to be content with a Christian community that neither is nor aims to be coextensive with the whole world order. They differ from early Calvinism both in their conception of what Christianity involves and in their choice of ways and means of seeking its embodiment in the institutional life of the world.

As these Christians see it, the existing structure of society, which embodies the principle of selfish competition for private gain, is not good enough. Not only does it occasionally blow up in a war and then break down in a depression; it persistently offers terrific obstacles to the development of the Christian character and to the practice of the Christian ethic. Therefore, they feel called of God to labor for a society that will embody, at least to some notable degree, the Christian principle of unselfish co-operation for the common good of all. And they further suppose that only as they do labor for such a society can they hope to develop in themselves the mind of Christ.

Surely, we are bound to affirm the right of God, through Jesus Christ, to rule over the whole domain of human life. Not to affirm it is to invite disaster. When national policy and economic practice are supposed to constitute a world over which religion and ethics have no jurisdiction, when they are permitted to develop laws of their own, as also ambitions and tempers, that have no regard for God and his righteousness, the result is bound to be what now we see—a world on the brink of an all-engulfing disaster. Nor is tragedy averted in the inner life of the individual. It strikes at the very soul of a man who ventures to suppose that his religion has nothing to do with his business. In health, the human self cannot be divided into two compartments—one in which God is recognized, another in which God is ignored. Only in disease may the self be thus divided. A man who should seriously persist in the attempt both to recognize God and to ignore God would become a "split personality." Few people, of course, do go so far as that; it is so much easier to resolve the tension by letting one's "recognition" of God become nothing more than a form of words. But this means that religion, which ought to be the greatest, has become the most petty thing in the world; and that the man who has made it so has himself become "as sounding brass or a tinkling cymbal."

Christians are bound to give attention to the external setting of their lives, unless they are content to let a situation develop in which the only alternative to awful acceptance of naked paganism, not to say diabolism, is the horror of a concentration camp. And such contentment would itself be an awful betrayal of Jesus Christ.

The kingdom of God is the gift of God, as is life itself and all that supports it. Yet we human creatures are not mere pawns unwittingly moved from place to place on a historic chessboard. The way of God in history is through men. It calls for men's understanding of His nature and purpose. It calls for men's appreciation of His truth and righteousness and love. It calls for men's unswerving devotion to His kingdom in heaven and on earth.

A PRAYER

Almighty and everlasting God, before whom pass the generations of men in triumph or in disaster, it comforts us to know that thou art concerned with all that concerns us and that in thy hands, not ours alone, are the issues of history. In days of tumult and peril, suffer us not to forget that thou art with us and that thou, O Lord, art able to do exceeding abundantly above all that we ask or think.

Reveal unto us the good in others that we are failing to see; that we may not despise our human clay nor ever suppose that human conditions, however bad, are irredeemable. And do thou in mercy reveal unto us the evil in ourselves; that we may not, with eyes in the ends of the earth, overlook much in our own desires and practices which is adding to the confusion and despair of the world.

We thank thee for the hope which now is ours that a way may yet be found out of the valley of the shadow of death. Show us, we beseech thee, the way that leads to life and to all for which, at our best, we care and hope and strive. Grant that we, seeing the awful futility of war, may now renounce everything that makes for war; and that, earnestly desiring peace, we may also desire those things which make for peace. Help us to do justly, to love mercy, and to walk humbly with thee.

By the awful need of the world, by the prayers of the noble dead, by thine own unending travail and pain, move us, we beseech thee, to commit ourselves wholly unto thee, that thy kingdom may come and thy will be done in earth as it is in heaven; through Jesus Christ our Lord. Amen.